FIRST
BIOGRAPHIES

Christopher Columbus

Trade Edition published 1995 © Steck-Vaughn Company.
© Copyright 1995 Steck-Vaughn Company.

Published by Raintree Steck-Vaughn Publishers, an imprint of Steck-Vaughn Company

Retold for young readers by Edith Vann
Editor: Pam Wells
Project Manager: Julie Klaus
Electronic Production: Scott Melcer

Library of Congress Cataloging-in-Publication Data

Gleiter, Jan, 1947-
    Christopher Columbus / by Jan Gleiter and Kathleen Thompson; illustrated by Rick Whipple.
      p.   cm. — (First biographies)
    ISBN 0-8114-8456-4 hardcover library binding
    ISBN 0-8114-9351-2 softcover binding
    1. Columbus, Christopher — Juvenile literature.   2. Explorers — America — Biography — Juvenile literature.   3. Explorers — Spain — Biography — Juvenile literature.   [1. Columbus, Christopher.
2. Explorers.   3. America — Discovery and exploration — Spanish.]
I. Thompson, Kathleen.   II. Whipple, Rick, ill.   III. Title.   IV. Series.
E111.G55   1995
970.01'5'092 — dc20   94-41003
[B]   CIP   AC

Printed and bound in the United States
  4 5 6 7 8 9 0 W 99

FIRST BIOGRAPHIES

Christopher Columbus

Jan Gleiter and Kathleen Thompson
Illustrated by Rick Whipple

RSVP
RAINTREE
STECK-VAUGHN
PUBLISHERS
The Steck-Vaughn Company

Austin, Texas

The boy stood high up on the ship's ropes. He was looking for land.

"Fernando! Boy! Roll up that sail!" a sailor shouted.

Fernando did it quickly. It was hard because he was small. On this ship boys did men's work. Fernando started down the ropes.

The ship suddenly rolled to one side. The boy's feet slid off the ropes. He held on with his hands to keep from falling. Then he climbed down fast before the ship rocked again.

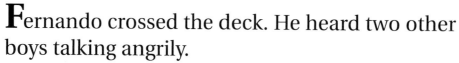

Fernando crossed the deck. He heard two other boys talking angrily.

"We would be on land," said one. "If it wasn't for that old goat, Columbus!"

"The men are ready to do something about him," the other said. "I'm ready to help."

Fernando stepped closer. "I wouldn't," he said. "And I'd watch what I said about the admiral."

"Like father, like son," the first boy laughed. "Do you want the men to take over this ship? Just tell your father to watch out."

7

Fernando went below deck. He didn't want to make his father worry. Yet his father must know what he had heard.

The admiral, Christopher Columbus, was writing a letter. He stopped and listened to his son.

"Father, you know I'll fight beside you," said the boy.

Columbus smiled. "So the men want a new leader! This isn't the first time. I can take care of them. Thank you for trying to help me. But thirteen-year-old boys should not have to fight for their fathers."

Christopher Columbus did know what to do. His men had tried to take over the ship before. In the past they had always lost these fights. They lost this one, too.

Columbus was not an easy man to work for. He could steer a ship by the stars. He could find his way across seas he did not know. This man was brave and clever. But Columbus had his own way of doing things. He didn't listen to others. He was probably the greatest sailor of his time. Fernando believed in him, too.

Columbus loved to tell his son stories about his travels. He told about the lands he had discovered. Fernando liked these stories.

A few nights later they stood together on deck. A cool wind was blowing. Fernando said, "Tell me about your first trip to the New World."

"Now, let me see," said Columbus. "That was a long time ago—ten years ago. I don't know if I remember it well enough."

Fernando laughed. He knew that his father remembered everything about it. After all, he had found a whole new world.

"**S**tart at the very beginning, Father," said
Fernando. "Tell me about going to the king and
queen of Spain. You needed money for the trip."

"Ah," said Columbus. "First I went to King John II
of Portugal. He had the best ships and sailors. I
needed good men and good ships because I had
a great idea."

"You knew you could get to the Indies by sea," said Fernando. He knew the story so well.

India, China, the East Indies, and Japan were called the Indies then. They lay far to the east. These faraway places had gold, spices, silk, and jewels. It was a long, hard trip by land. Everyone wanted a quicker way to get there.

"I was quite sure my way would work," his father said. "I knew the best and fastest way to get to the East was to sail ..."

"West!" shouted Fernando.

"**Y**es," Columbus said. He touched his son's right ear. "This is Europe." Then he touched the left ear. "This is the Indies. I could walk east over all this land." He moved his finger across Fernando's nose. "Or because the world is round, I could sail west." He moved his hand across the back of his son's head. He grabbed his left ear. "Ah, ha! The Indies!"

16

"**K**ing John didn't believe you?" asked Fernando.

"Oh, he knew the world was round," said Columbus. "But he had men who knew a lot to help him. They were wise. In fact, they thought they knew best where to find the Indies."

"And the king listened to them, instead of you," Fernando said.

"That's right," said his father. "He listened to them." Suddenly he laughed. "I guess they are angry with themselves over in Portugal right now!"

"Maybe the king was mad at them, too, when he heard your news." Fernando's eyes were bright.

"Oh, you never know about kings. Or queens," said Columbus.

"So you went to Spain. You saw King Ferdinand and Queen Isabella," said his son. "Then what happened?"

19

"I went to them again and again," said Columbus. "I made maps. I asked and asked. They thought I wanted too much money and power. Then they said yes. I sailed with three ships and ninety men in August of 1492."

"You sailed and sailed," said Fernando. "On the *Niña,* the *Pinta,* and the *Santa Maria.*"

"Yes," said his father. "At first the men were excited. But weeks went by with no sight of land. They were afraid. The wind kept blowing us west. They thought we couldn't get home again."

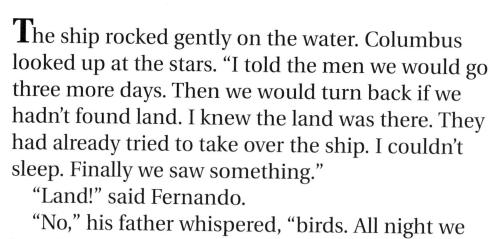

The ship rocked gently on the water. Columbus looked up at the stars. "I told the men we would go three more days. Then we would turn back if we hadn't found land. I knew the land was there. They had already tried to take over the ship. I couldn't sleep. Finally we saw something."

"Land!" said Fernando.

"No," his father whispered, "birds. All night we heard them. The next morning we saw lots of birds. They were flying toward the southwest. I told my men to follow the birds—southwest."

"Then, no one could sleep at night," said Fernando softly. "Suddenly the lookout shouted when he saw land."

"Land, at last," said Columbus. "It wasn't just any place we saw in the moonlight. It was a new world!"

"We went onto the shore," Columbus said. "The people who lived there met us and gave us gifts. I named the place San Salvador."

The "Indies" Columbus had found were not the Indies. He believed he was near China or Japan. He was really in the Bahama Islands, southeast of Florida. He never knew how wrong he was. He had really landed near a large mass of land that Europe knew nothing about. He had done something much more important than he had ever dreamed.

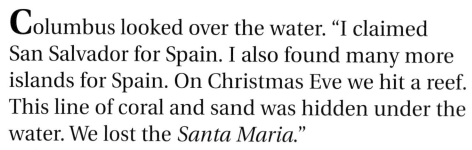

Columbus looked over the water. "I claimed San Salvador for Spain. I also found many more islands for Spain. On Christmas Eve we hit a reef. This line of coral and sand was hidden under the water. We lost the *Santa Maria*."

"You almost didn't make it home. Is that true, Father?"

"On our way back the storms were very bad," said Columbus. "So I wrote down the story of my findings. I put it in a barrel made of wood. And I threw it into the water. I was afraid no one would ever know what I had found."

"**F**inally, you did return to Spain," said Fernando. He knew about his father's great honor. "The king and queen listened to all you had done! They gave you a title. It was Admiral of the Ocean Sea! Now we're going back to that New World."

"Yes, we're going back. I've been there three times. This time you will see it yourself. You'll see what I first saw ten years ago."

"I'll find gold to take home," said the boy. "And you'll make new discoveries!"

Later on that trip, Columbus had more problems. He had to search for food and a warm, dry, and safe place. He won again when his men tried to take over. He was in fights with those people he called "Indians." We call these first peoples Native Americans. Columbus and his men made it through many storms. Then the worms ate holes in their ships.

In the end, they made it home again. Years later Fernando would write about the trip. He would tell about his father, Christopher Columbus, Admiral of the Ocean Sea.

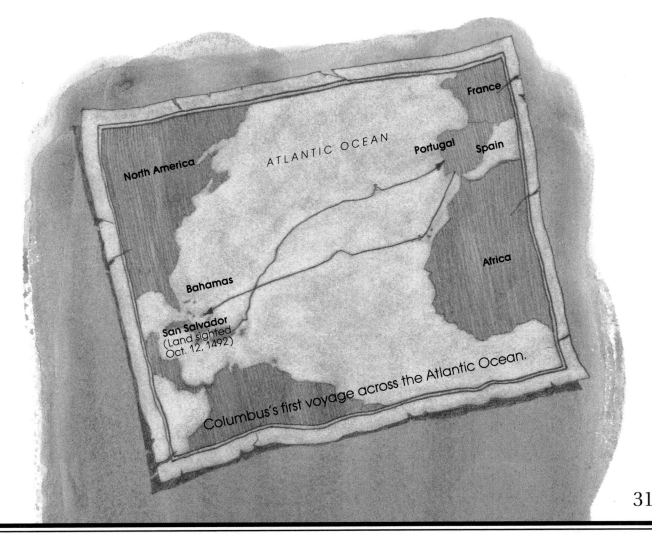

Columbus's first voyage across the Atlantic Ocean.

Key Dates

1451   Christopher Columbus is born in Genoa, an Italian seaport.

1471   Columbus goes to sea for the first time.

1477   Marries and has a son, Diego.

1482   Asks the king of Portugal for ships and men. Columbus wants to prove that the East could be reached by sailing west. He is refused.

1485   Takes his plan to the Spanish rulers and is again refused.

1492   At last, Queen Isabella of Spain agrees to his plan. On August 3, sails with three ships from Palos, Spain. On October 12, lands on the island of San Salvador in the Bahamas.

1493   Returns to his home, Palos, March 15.

Sets out on his second attempt to reach the East on September 25. Reaches the West Indies, November 3.

1498   Leaves on his third voyage May 30. He becomes the first European to set foot on mainland South America. Columbus believes it to be Southeast Asia.

1500   Columbus returns to Spain.

1502   Makes his fourth attempt to find a route to the Indies. His thirteen-year-old son, Fernando, goes with him.

1504   Returns to Spain, having failed in his search.

1506   Christopher Columbus dies on May 20.